Echoes of Resilience

A Poetic Guide to Hope & Purpose

Rebekah Hope

#You cantoo

Rebekah Hope

ACTIONS & FLOW MEDIA, LLC

Copyright © 2024 by Rebekah Hope

All rights reserved.

No portion of this book may be reproduced in any form without written permission from the publisher or author, except as permitted by U.S. copyright law.

Contents

Dedication	VII
Acknowledgements	VIII
1. Resilience	1
2. The Heart That Refuses to Fall	2
3. Tied to Chains No More	4
4. Wings of Resilience	7
5. Unshakable Spirit	10
6. Shattered but Whole	13
7. Unconsumed: She is the Fire	16
8. Born of Fire, Forged by Hope	19
9. Brave Enough to Begin	21
10. The Power Within	24
11. Fearlessly Forward	27

12.	Rise with Purpose	29
13.	Her True Identity	32
14.	The Lifeline Restored	34
15.	Unwavered	37
16.	Broken Roads Led Me Here	40
17.	Colors of the Marble	42
18.	The Power Within	45
19.	I Live to Tell	48
20.	Clothed in Strength	50
21.	Hope	53
22.	To Death I Wish No More	54
23.	Hope in Every Step	56
24.	Guided by Grace	59
25.	Destiny is Mine	62
26.	In Search of Hope	64
27.	Whispers from the Mountain	67
28.	Where Love Unbounds	70
29.	From Cocoon to Butterfly	73
30.	Passport to Heaven	75
31.	A Journey of Purpose	77
32.	Becoming Love	80
33.	50 Shades of Lipstick	83

34.	From the Skyline	86
35.	Kindness, Pass It On	89
36.	Brave Enough to Begin	91
37.	Tethered for Life: I Think Not	94
38.	In Overflow - A Forgotten Faucet	96
39.	Baggage Claim: Unchecked	99
40.	Faithful Voices: A Tribute from the Throne Room	102
41.	Personal Growth	105
42.	In the Moment, Not for the Moment	106
43.	Blooming into Womanhood	108
44.	Color me Purple	111
45.	New Name - Same Heart	113
46.	Finding my Fire	115
47.	Head in Cages	118
48.	Layers Unfolded	120
49.	Her Story, Her Strength	122
50.	Courageous Hearts	125
51.	Coffee No Cure	128
52.	I Hold My Tongue	130
53.	A Heart Forgiven – Peace Restored	132
54.	Daffodils So Bright	134
55.	The Swingset of Womanhood	136

56.	Keyboard of My Heart	139
57.	Days Gone By	141
58.	A Woman in Red	143
59.	Love's True Power: Still I Choose	146
60.	I Toyed with You	149
61.	I Made My Bed, Now What?	152
62.	Deal with the Devil: Canceled	155
63.	A Common Current	158
64.	In the Know	161
Afterword		164
About the author		166

This book is for every woman who needs to be reminded that she is resilient, she is worthy, and she has a purpose waiting to be found. As you read, may you feel the hope that stirred within me while writing, and may you know that your voice, your story, and your life truly matters.

Acknowledgements

First and foremost, I want to give thanks to my heavenly Father. When I opened my heart and surrendered to being a vessel for him, I knew these words weren't just mine. They were whispers from the Divine, flowing through me onto these pages. Without God's hand guiding me, there would be no book—just empty sheets. So I thank the Lord, not just for the words, but for trusting me to carry His message, for choosing me to pour out hope and healing to every woman who needs it. This book is a testimony of His grace, and I am honored to share it with you.

Secondly, I want to show my appreciation for my writing and book coach, Sha'viel Mckiver of Fierce Pen Writing and Coaching (fiercepencoaching@gmail.com) for her dedication to this book and to me as a writer. Collaborating with her is what made this book possible. She is truly gifted in her ability to coach individuals into professional writers and help them share their story. Words fall short in my appreciation for her role in getting this book into your hands. Thank you, Sha'viel for inspiring me, coaching me, and for all the behind-the-scenes work you did on this book. You are a true gift from God.

To my Community—From the heart of the author: Echoes of Resilience is more than just a collection of poems; it's a lifeline for women who feel lost, broken, or weary. Born out of my own journey through darkness and doubt, this book is a heartfelt offering to every woman who has ever questioned her worth or wondered why she's here. Each poem serves as a gentle whisper reminding you that you're not alone, that your struggles do not define you, and that even the most shattered pieces can be gathered and shaped into something beautiful.

These pages are filled with raw honesty, written for the woman who is desperately searching for meaning, for the woman who feels like she's just surviving instead of truly living. The poems reach out like a hand in the dark, inviting you to rise, to heal, and to find strength in the stories that echo within us all. They are about embracing flaws, finding courage to stand back up, and discovering the quiet power that grows in the midst of trials.

Contact Rebekah

Rebekah.DivineHope@gmail.com

Website: https://linktr.ee/rebekahhope

Join us on Facebook @Divine Hope Community

Resilience

THE STRENGTH TO RISE

Resilience is the strength to rise after every fall, and the courage to keep moving forward, even when the path is uncertain. It's the way we rebuild ourselves from brokenness, finding beauty in our scars, and embracing the journey of becoming whole again. This is for the women who've faced storms and still stand— stronger, wiser, and more true to themselves.

This section is dedicated to the battles we fight and the strength we discover along the way. These poems reflect the journey of falling and rising again, of finding courage within when all seems lost. Let these words remind you of the power you hold, and the beauty that comes from never giving up.

The Heart That Refuses to Fall

On days when the weight was too much to bear,

When doubt whispered lies, and life felt unfair.

Deep inside, there was a fire burning bright,

A heart that refused to give up the fight.

She's been knocked down, broken, and bruised,

Faced with a world that often refused.

But even in moments when darkness would call,

She stood with a heart that refused to fall.

Through tears, through storms, she found her way,

Knowing tomorrow could bring a better day.

Each scar she carried told stories of grace,

Of rising again, no matter the pace.

The world may not see the battles she's won,

The silent victories, the races she's run.

But she knows her strength, the power inside,

A heart full of courage that's never denied.

So here she stands, unshaken, whole,

With purpose ignited deep in her soul.

For every step forward, for every tall wall,

She is the heart that refuses to fall

Tied to Chains No More

Bound by chains that I couldn't see,

A life controlled, not meant for me.

They held the keys, they ruled my days,

But deep inside, I knew my ways.

I dreamed of skies where I could fly,

Of open doors, and reaching high.

Though they had power over my will,

My spirit fought, my heart stood still.

Each whispered "no" became my fire,

A quiet strength, a fierce desire.

To break the hold, to claim my name,

To live my life without the shame.

The chains are gone, I stand up tall,

I've learned to rise after each fall.

My voice is mine, my path is bright,

No more control, I embrace the light.

The life I lead is truly my own,

A single mind, a heart full-grown.

An entrepreneur, with dreams in hand,

I've built my life, I've made my stand.

From deep shadows, I've found the sun,

With every step, my journey's begun.

The world is vast, and I am free,

To live the life that's meant for me.

The world may not see the battles she's won,

The silent victories, the races she's run.

But she knows her strength, the power inside,

A heart full of courage that's never denied.

So here she stands, unshaken, whole,

With purpose ignited deep in her soul.

For every step forward, for every tall wall,

She is the heart that refuses to fall.

Wings of Resilience

In the quiet dawn of her youth's early light,

She faced the seasons, dark and bright.

Through winter's chill and summer's blaze,

Her spirit soared through every phase.

Spring brought hope with its tender touch,

Yet, she battled storms that raged too much.

Each change, each challenge, she embraced,

With a heart that never lost its grace.

Autumn leaves fell, and with them, fears,

But she spread her wings, despite the tears.

For every trial, every shifting wind,

Was a lesson learned, a strength to win.

Through every season, harsh or mild,

She remained the resilient, fierce-hearted child.

Her wings grew stronger, and her light shone clear,

A beacon of hope for all who drew near.

From the darkest nights to the sunlit skies,

Her courage glittered in the world's eyes.

For she emerged from every storm and scar,

Shining brighter than any distant star.

Now she soars with a radiant grace,

Unbound by the trials she's faced.

In every season, her spirit's been the guide,

Wings of resilience spread far and wide.

With each new dawn, her light will gleam,

A testament to the strength that beams.

For in the heart of the one who fought and tried,

Lives the star that lights the night sky wide.

Unshakable Spirit

In the darkest of nights, she walked alone,

With a heart that was shattered, strength overthrown.

Loved ones betrayed her, leaving scars so deep,

Yet her spirit endured, as the world made her weep.

They took what they could—her joy, her trust,

Reduced her to ashes, turned dreams into dust.

But deep inside, where no hand could reach,

Her unshakable spirit held on to hope's speech.

For though the pain felt too heavy to bear,

She knew Jesus stood with her, always there.

His light broke through in the harshest of times,

Guiding her heart through the relentless climb.

They couldn't steal what they couldn't see,

The faith she held in eternity.

Her spirit, unbroken, though battered and bruised,

Stood firm in the love that never refused.

In Christ alone, she found her strength,

He carried her through the endless length,

Of suffering, loss, and deep despair,

Until she discovered peace, beyond compare.

They took everything, but they couldn't take Him,

The source of her hope when all seemed dim.

And through the fire, she emerged whole,

With Jesus restoring her wounded soul.

Now she stands, unshakable still,

Her spirit forged by her Savior's will.

For though the world tried to tear her apart,

Christ healed her wounds and renewed her heart.

No longer bound by what was lost,

She walks in freedom, counting the cost.

Her unshakable spirit, a beacon of grace,

Living proof of God's embrace.

So let the storms come, let the winds blow,

She stands with Christ, and she'll always know—

That no matter what comes, no matter what's done,

Her unshakable spirit has already won.

Shattered but Whole

In the stillness of night, when the world feels immense,

Life hit hard, and the die was cast.

She watched as her dreams shattered like glass,

Each fragment is a reminder of moments that pass.

Her heart felt heavy, weighed down by pain,

In the ruins of hope, she sought something to gain.

Yet amidst the turmoil, a truth began to bloom,

In breaking apart, she could find room.

For in every fracture, there lay a new spark,

A glimpse of her spirit igniting the dark.

She learned that the pieces once seen as her loss,

Were pathways to freedom, a bridge through the gloss.

With courage, she gathered each glimmering shard,

Embracing the lessons, though the journey was hard.

What once felt like ruin transformed into art,

A mosaic of strength pieced together with heart.

She discovered in her shattering a beauty so rare,

The essence of wholeness was hidden with care.

For had she not stumbled, had she not come apart,

She would never have known the fullness of her heart.

So let life take its course, let the chips fall away,

For in every unraveling, new colors will play.

When the storms of existence try to tear you in two,

Remember, dear sister, the wholeness is you.

In shattered times, rise like a phoenix in flight,

Embrace the new dawn, step into the light.

For the you that emerges, raw, radiant, bold,

Is the truest reflection of the life you were sold.

So shatter and sparkle, let your spirit unfold,

In becoming all broken, you're finally whole.

Each step that you take, know the journey's the goal,

For in every new fracture, you find the real soul.

Unconsumed: She is the Fire

In the furnace of trials, where shadows loom,

She walks through the flames, trusting He'll make room.

"For when you pass through waters, I will be near,"

(Isaiah 43:2) whispers of hope, silencing her fear.

The fire may burn, but it will not consume,

Like Shadrach, Meshach, and Abednego's tunes.

In the heart of the blaze, there's One by her side,

A Savior, a Friend, in whom she can confide.

"For I know the plans I have for you," says the Lord,

Plans to prosper, to hope, and to restore.

(Jeremiah 29:11) her heart clings tight,

In every dark hour, He's her guiding light.

When trials arise, and burdens feel great,

"Cast all your cares on Him" (1 Peter 5:7) – He's never late.

He refines like silver, through fire and pain,

A promise of growth, through loss and gain.

So she lifts her eyes, through smoke and despair,

With faith as her armor, she breathes in the air.

"For God has not given a spirit of fear,"

(2 Timothy 1:7) she proclaims with cheer.

With every heartbeat, her purpose shines bright,

"Fearfully and wonderfully made" (Psalm 139:14), she ignites.

Through the fire, she rises, a beacon of grace,

Transforming her trials into sacred space.

And as the flames flicker, she stands tall and free,

"For in all things, she is more than a conqueror" (Romans 8:37), you see.

With courage, she walks, through the fire's fierce glow,

A testimony of faith, with each step she'll grow.

Born of Fire, Forged by Hope

In the heart of the flames, where shadows sway,

She stood with courage, ready to seize the day.

From the fiery trials that scorched her core,

Rose is a spirit resilient, awake and wanting more.

Born from the fire that tested her will,

She emerged with strength, her heart now filled.

Each ember a lesson, each blaze a guide,

Forged by hope, she learned to take pride.

Through the smoke and the heat, she learned to rise,

Her heart grew bolder, reaching for the skies.

In life's trials, where fears intertwine,

She carved her own path, each victory divine.

Her spirit, like steel, strong and aglow,

Shines with a light that cuts through the shadow.

For in the heart of the flames, she found her way,

A true beacon of hope, come what may.

Born of the fire, yet not lost in its blaze,

She dances with purpose through dark and bright days.

Her wings of resilience spread wide and free,

Forged by hope, she's living proof that dreams can be.

Brave Enough to Begin

She stood at the edge, bound by invisible chains,

In a world shaped by culture, tradition's reign.

They urged her to stay, to follow the line,

But deep in her heart, she sensed a sign.

For too long she'd adhered to the rules they laid,

Trapped by expectations that never seemed to fade.

Yet a fire within her started to ignite,

Whispering softly, "You were meant for more than this fight."

It wasn't in customs or traditions' hold,

Her hope, her purpose, they couldn't uphold.

In a realm of restrictions, she'd never discover
The freedom her spirit longed to uncover.

But with courage swelling, she took that leap,
Brave enough to abandon the life she'd keep.
Shattering the chains not just for her own,
But for countless others who felt all alone.

She walked toward freedom, toward the dawn,
With Jesus as her guide, she felt reborn.
In Him, she found the meaning she sought,
For it was in Christ her battles were fought.

Tradition grew quiet, culture lost its sway,
As she moved in freedom, day by day.
No longer shackled by the world's demands,
She entrusted her life into His loving hands.

And in that moment, she came to see,
Hope had never resided in what others decree.

It wasn't in the norms that held her down,

But in Jesus Christ, where her strength was found.

She was brave enough to start the fight,

Brave enough to step into the light.

And with each stride, she forged a path,

For others to find freedom, to feel the aftermath.

So to you, dear sister, who stands at the brink,

Know that freedom thrives in the heart that dares to think.

Be brave enough to take that first stride,

For in Christ alone, your purpose will abide.

The Power Within

The world may tell you how to live,

What to take and what to give.

It whispers that you're not enough,

That life is hard, the road is tough.

But hear me now, and hear it clear:

The power you need is already here.

It's not in the voices outside your door,

It's deep in your heart, it's what you're made for.

You don't need to follow someone else's way,

Or bend to the rules they force you to obey.

The path you seek, the dream you chase,

Live in the courage that you embrace.

You hold the strength, the power, the fire,

To create the life that you desire.

It's not found in their plans, their rules, their voice,

It's found in your heart, your soul, your choice.

So, trust yourself, take the lead,

You are the captain, you plant the seed.

No more waiting for someone to show

Which way to turn, or where to go.

The power is within, it's always been,

In every loss and every win.

In every choice you dare to make,

In every risk you choose to take.

You hold the keys to your own fate,

To rise above, it's never too late.

So walk with purpose, and trust the light,

That shines within, and gives you sight.

The world may shake, but you'll stand tall,

For you've found the strength beneath it all.

And with each step, you'll boldly see,

The power within sets you free.

Fearlessly Forward

I stand at the edge, the world laid out wide,

With dreams in my heart and a fire deep inside.

Every moment a chance to take a bold leap,

Fearlessly forward, with hope that I keep.

The road may be rough, the path often dark,

But I cling to my courage, igniting the spark.

For each step I take, even when the way's unclear,

I trust in the journey, my spirit sincere.

I keep my focus sharp, my eyes on the goal,

Knowing each little step brings me closer, makes me whole.

One day at a time, one breath, one beat,

I find my direction, my heart skips a beat.

With kindness as armor and love as my guide,

I navigate shadows, learning to abide.

Each challenge a lesson, each stumble a part,

Of the beautiful dance that awakens my heart.

I may not have all the answers right now,

But I'm learning that life is a wondrous vow.

With each step I take, I uncover the way,

I'm finding my path, and I'm here to stay.

So onward I go, with strength in my core,

For I know that the journey is what I adore.

Fearlessly forward, I rise and I thrive,

In the light of my purpose, I'm truly alive.

Rise with Purpose

When the weight of the world feels heavy and cold,

And you wonder if you'll break or be bold,

Remember, dear sister, you're stronger than you know,

In the heart of the storm is where you'll grow.

Don't wait for the skies to clear their gray,

Don't wait for the perfect, sunny day.

Right where you are, in the middle of the fight,

Is where you'll discover your greatest light.

It's easy to think that purpose will come,

When the battle is over, when the struggle is done.

But purpose is found in the hardest parts,

It's born from the courage deep in your heart.

Rise with purpose, even when it's tough,

When life feels too heavy, when it's all too much.

You don't have to wait for the pain to cease,

You can find your strength and make your peace.

In every step you take through fire and rain,

You're shaping your future, you're breaking the chain.

You'll rise from the ashes, brighter than before,

With a heart full of purpose, ready for more.

So stand up tall, even when you feel small,

There's a reason you're here, you're meant to stand tall.

Your story's unfolding, and in every test,

You'll find that your purpose is rising, blessed.

You're more than your struggle, more than your fear,

You're a warrior of hope, and your purpose is near.

So rise, dear sister, right where you stand,

With courage in your heart and purpose in hand.

Her True Identity

In the stillness of her spirit, she starts to explore,

Not in the world, but in Christ, whom she adores.

"Who am I?" she cries, her heart open wide,

The answer gently comes, with love as her guide.

"For you are a chosen people, a royal priesthood," He speaks,

1 Peter 2:9, her heart begins to seek.

No longer lost, no longer in doubt,

In Christ, she discovers what life is about.

In Ephesians 2:10, she recognizes her design,

"For we are God's handiwork," beautifully aligned.

Created for good, with a purpose to fulfill,

Through Him, she finds strength and the will.

She's no longer shackled by the weight of her past,

2 Corinthians 5:17 assures, "the old has passed."

A new creation, with each dawn a fresh start,

In Christ alone, she'll follow her heart.

So she walks in His light, with poise and with grace,

Knowing in Him, she's found her rightful place.

"I am fearfully and wonderfully made," she declares,

Psalm 139:14 forever in her prayers.

Now, she stands tall, embracing her call,

Not glancing back, but giving Him her all.

In Christ, she's complete, no longer confined,

Her identity revealed, her purpose aligned.

The Lifeline Restored

In the shadows of hatred, where darkness took its hold,

A lifeline once untouched, left her story untold.

Evil whispered softly, planting seeds of despair,

But deep within her spirit, a flicker still laid bare.

With each cruel cut and tether, the lifeline frayed and wore,

She felt the grip of anguish, a weight she could not ignore.

Yet, in the depths of silence, a whisper broke the night,

"Dear heart, I'm not finished; hold on to the light."

God watched from above, His love steadfast and true,

He summoned forth His angels, sending strength anew.

With wings of gentle comfort, they soared through the air,

Restoring the lifeline, a rescue beyond compare.

Once severed and alone, now intertwined once more,

Connected to a power that opened every door.

No longer just a victim of all that had transpired,

She felt the pulse of courage, igniting her desire.

The lifeline sparkled brightly, like stars against the dark,

It pulsed with holy promise, igniting every spark.

With every breath she took, she felt the strength arise,

Her spirit soared unshackled, as she claimed her rightful skies.

For evil could not bind her; it could not hold her fast,

With angels by her side, she knew her fate was cast.

The lifeline was a beacon, a testament of grace,

In the journey of her healing, she found her rightful place.

Now tethered to her purpose, she walks a path so clear,

With love and light surrounding, she casts away her fear.

For every trial faced, every tear she had to shed,

Became the very fabric of the strength in which she tread.

So let it be a lesson, for those who've lost their way:

A lifeline can be mended, even in dismay.

God's angels guard the broken, their love a timeless thread,

And in the arms of hope, our truest selves are bred.

Unwavered

Once she felt trapped by invisible chains,

A captive heart, yet still a queen.

In silence, she stood, as doubt drew near,

But her soul whispered, "Do not fear."

The world pressed hard, the weight was real,

Yet deep within, she chose to heal.

For she knew her worth was never lost,

Her strength was there, guiding her across.

Her crown wasn't made of gold or jewels,

But forged in faith, unshaken by fools.

Though trials came like storms in the night,

She held her ground, a warrior in light.

Though waters rose and fires burned,

Her heart remained strong, the tides were turned.

No force on earth could crush her soul,

Her spirit soared, she stayed whole.

She was a queen, though captive still,

Her spirit fierce, her iron will.

For freedom, she knew, was not just sight,

But found in truth, in endless light.

In the mirror, she saw what others missed—

A woman of purpose, beautifully kissed.

By grace, by love, by strength untold,

A queen unwavered, beautiful and bold.

So to every sister, bound or free,

Remember your power, your identity.

You are a queen, no matter the fight,

Rise with purpose, and shine with light.

Broken Roads Led Me Here

The broken roads I've traveled, each winding and steep,

Have carved out my story, the secrets I keep.

With every stumble and each tear I shed,

I found strength in the struggles, in the words left unsaid.

I wandered through shadows, felt lost in the dark,

But the flicker of hope ignited a spark.

Each detour and dead end whispered to me,

That the path of my journey was setting me free.

The cracks in my heart told tales of despair,

But from those very fractures, I learned how to care.

With each jagged edge, I discovered my worth,

In the rubble of heartache, I found my rebirth.

These broken roads led me to lessons profound,

In the moments of silence, my voice could be found.

The scars that I carry are maps of my fight,

Guiding me forward, embracing the light.

So here I stand, with a heart open wide,

Grateful for journeys where I learned to abide.

The broken roads have shaped me, it's true,

And in every misstep, I've grown into you.

Colors of the Marble

In life, we see the marbles shine,

Each one a color, each one a sign.

They glimmer bright, they catch our eye,

Trying to pull us from our why.

There's red for anger, blue for fear,

Green for envy that draws us near.

Yellow for doubt that clouds the way,

Purple for pride that leads astray.

These colors swirl, they seem so bright,

They distract us from our truest light.

But look again, and you will find,

They hold no power over your mind.

For each one's just a marble, small and round,

A fleeting thing, not solid ground.

They cannot weigh your spirit down,

Nor take away your rightful crown.

Though they try to make you trip and fall,

They're just reflections—nothing at all.

Pick them up, don't let them stay,

Place them in the jar, and walk away.

For in that jar, they sit confined,

Their colors fade, their power declined.

No longer distractions, no longer chains,

They are but marbles, with no true gains.

They make the jar look full, it's true,

But they can't decide what's best for you.

Your purpose shines beyond their hue,

A light within that's always new.

So gather each one, don't be afraid,

They're just the colors life has made.

But they hold no weight, they cannot steer,

When your purpose in Christ is crystal clear.

Now walk your path, don't be deceived,

By colors bright that once deceived.

For marbles may be pretty things,

But they won't stop what your heart brings.

Pick them up, and put them away,

In the jar, they'll stay at bay.

For you are meant for greater things,

To walk in purpose, on your wings.

The Power Within

The world may tell you how to live,

What to take and what to give.

It whispers that you're not enough,

That life is hard, the road is tough.

But hear me now, and hear it clear:

The power you need is already here.

It's not in the voices outside your door,

It's deep in your heart, it's what you're made for.

You don't need to follow someone else's way,

Or bend to the rules they force you to obey.

The path you seek, the dream you chase,

Lives in the courage that you embrace.

You hold the strength, the power, the fire,

To create the life that you desire.

It's not found in their plans, their rules, their voice,

It's found in your heart, your soul, your choice.

So, trust yourself, take the lead,

You are the captain, you plant the seed.

No more waiting for someone to show

Which way to turn, or where to go.

The power is within, it's always been,

In every loss and every win.

In every choice you dare to make,

In every risk you choose to take.

You hold the keys to your own fate,

To rise above, it's never too late.

So walk with purpose, and trust the light,

That shines within, and gives you sight.

The world may shake, but you'll stand tall,

For you've found the strength beneath it all.

And with each step, you'll boldly see,

The power within sets you free.

I Live to Tell

I've walked through fires, felt the burn,

Faced the storm with no way to return.

The weight of darkness pressed me low,

But deep inside, a light would glow.

I've stumbled through shadows, feeling lost,

Paid the price, no matter the cost.

Yet even when the night felt long,

I found my strength, I found my song.

Bruised but not broken, torn yet whole,

Life tried to crush, but not my soul.

Through every tear, through every fall,

I rise again—I've answered the call.

I live to tell of battles won,

To speak of hope when all seems done.

I stand to show the scars I bear,

For they are proof I'm still standing here.

No chains of fear, no voice of doubt

Will ever turn my spirit out.

I live to tell, I live to fight,

And through it all, I find my light.

With every breath, with every scar,

I'll shine to show just who we are—

Strong, unshaken, bold and free,

Living proof of victory.

Clothed in Strength

She is wrapped in strength and dignity, that much is true,

For the Lord has made her heart feel brand new.

As Proverbs 31:25 reminds us,

She laughs without fear, for God knows her trust.

When storms arise and the waves crash high,

She holds His promise: Isaiah 41:10 close by.

"Fear not, for I am with you," He gently speaks,

In her moments of weakness, His power peaks.

With each step she takes, Psalm 46:5 lights her way,

"God is within her; she won't fall," come what may.

Though the road may be tough, and her burdens feel great,

She stands firm, trusting in her God-given fate.

Jeremiah 29:11, she keeps in her heart,

"For I know the plans I have for you," He imparts.

Plans to prosper, to give hope and a future,

In His love, she finds her truest nature.

As she walks this path, she clings to the light,

Knowing Romans 8:28 will make things right.

"All things work together for good,"

Even when she couldn't see it, He understood.

With faith like a mustard seed, she moves the hills,

Her trust in the Lord is what truly fulfills.

Philippians 4:13 is her daily refrain:

"I can do all things through Christ," in joy and in pain.

So, rise up, dear sister, in the strength you've been given,

For you are loved, cherished, and completely forgiven.

With the Word as your sword and His love as your shield,

In Christ, you're victorious; your future is sealed.

Hope

A Light in the Darkness

Hope is the light that flickers even in the darkest moments, the quiet belief that better days are always possible. It's the steady reminder that no matter how heavy the present feels, tomorrow holds the promise of something new. For those who have felt lost, hope is the whisper that guides you back to yourself, urging you to trust in the future and in your own unfolding story.

Here you will find poems that speak to the quiet belief in better days, the faith in something brighter beyond the present moment. As you turn these pages, may you feel a sense of renewal, a spark of hope that fuels your spirit and keeps you moving forward.

To Death I Wish No More

I once stood at the edge of night,

Chasing shadows, avoiding light.

A heart so worn, it yearned for peace,

In darkness deep, it found no ease.

Caught in the grip of endless pain,

It seemed that peace wasn't worth the strain.

The world felt cold, and dreams were thin,

The end of life seemed like the only win.

Yet I lifted my eyes to future's bright,

A radiant beacon in the fading night.

I felt the power deep within my core,

Even when pain was all I bore.

I could reshape the path I'd trod,

And leave behind the shadows, flawed.

No longer bound by darkness' snare,

I spread my wings and breathed fresh air.

My heart, once bruised, beats strong and clear,

Spreading hope to those who chose to hear.

Embracing life with an open heart,

Joy and love playing their part.

From the dark of night to this vibrant place,

I share my journey, my healing grace.

In every moment, I've found the way,

To live fully, come what may.

My spirit's strength, a guiding light,

Shows how resilience turns the night.

Hope in Every Step

They attempted to take what wasn't theirs to keep,

To steal the good and make the heart weep.

But through the storms, she walked without fear,

For her hope in the Lord would always be near.

The winds howled fiercely, the skies turned dark,

Yet her spirit stood strong, igniting a spark.

For deep inside, where no harm could invade,

Her soul found a hope that would never fade.

It wasn't in the things they sought to claim,

Not in what the world could twist or maim.

But in Christ alone, she found her peace,

In His unwavering love, she found release.

Every step she took through the longest night,

She clung to hope, her shining light.

The storms may have raged, but they couldn't reach

The calm she held in God's love, a powerful speech.

No matter the lies or the trials they threw,

She walked in hope, with faith guiding her view.

Her eyes set on the truth that lasts,

That the Lord was her anchor, her steadfast cast.

When others stumbled, when all seemed bleak,

She remembered the One who was strong when weak.

And in Him, her hope would never bend,

Even when the storm refused to end.

They couldn't take from her what she held dear,

The hope that remained, steady and clear.

For no matter how fiercely the winds would blow,

Her hope in the Lord would only grow.

With every step, she chose to rise,

Untouched by the world, with faith in her eyes.

The louder the storm, the clearer her sight,

Focused on hope, walking in light.

Now she stands, unyielding, secure,

A heart full of hope, steadfast and pure.

For in every step, through joy and through strife,

She discovered her hope, her purpose, her life.

And though the world tried to break her apart,

They couldn't touch the depths of her heart.

For in Christ alone, her hope was found,

And in His love, she was forever bound.

Guided by Grace

When life takes unexpected turns,

And you find yourself asking, "Why me?"

When the weight of the world feels too heavy to carry,

And you're searching for hope, but it seems so far away.

Remember, dear heart, in the midst of it all,

There's a grace that will catch you, even when you fall.

It's not just in the sunshine or only in the good,

But in every season, right where you've stood.

Grace isn't something you earn; it's a gift from above,

It softly reminds you of the power of love.

Through all the chaos, confusion, and pain,

Grace is the calm that comes with the rain.

When nothing feels right and life seems unfair,

When the world feels overwhelming, and you're gasping for air,

Let grace be your guide, let it light your way,

Through the darkest of nights and the toughest of days.

You don't need to be perfect or have it all figured out,

Grace will hold you gently, easing your doubt.

It will lead you through every stumble and tear,

Reminding you always, there's nothing to fear.

For even in trouble, even in doubt,

Grace is the path that will pull you out.

So trust in the journey, though rough it may seem,

Grace will guide you, and soon you'll dream.

That every tough moment is shaping your soul,

And through it, you're learning, becoming whole.

So walk with grace, with your head held high,

You'll rise from this season, and learn how to fly.

Guided by grace, you'll find your way,

Through the storm, you'll grow stronger each day.

And when you look back, you'll see how you've grown,

With grace as your guide, you were never alone.

Destiny is Mine

In the quiet of morning, with dreams in my heart,

I rise with a fire, ready to start.

The world lies before me, a canvas so wide,

And I know at this moment, I won't run and hide.

No longer a whisper of doubt in my mind,

I step into purpose, leaving fear behind.

With every decision, I carve out my way,

For destiny beckons, and I choose to stay.

I embrace all my struggles, the lessons they teach,

Each stumble is a stepping stone, just within reach.

I gather my courage, I hold my head high,

With faith as my anchor, I'm ready to fly.

The road may be winding, the path not yet clear,

But I trust in the journey, and I cast aside fear.

For I am the author, the maker of dreams,

With strength in my spirit, I burst at the seams.

I claim my tomorrow, I shape it today,

With passion and purpose, I'll light up the way.

For destiny's calling, it's louder somehow,

And I'm ready to answer—I will seize it right now.

So here in this moment, I rise and I stand,

With hope in my heart and the world in my hand.

Destiny is mine, I'm ready to show,

That the power to flourish is all that I know.

In Search of Hope

In the stillness of your heart, where whispers reside,

God's love calls gently, a truth to confide.

Jeremiah 29:11, His plans are revealed,

A future filled with hope, a promise unsealed.

When life feels burdensome, and shadows draw near,

He reassures, "Fear not, my child, I am here."

Isaiah 41:10, His strength is your shield,

With every step forward, let go of your fear.

Though challenges arise, like storms that may roar,

Romans 8:28 speaks of something more.

For all things work together, a divine design,

In your moments of weakness, His strength will align.

Ephesians 2:10, you're made with intent,

A masterpiece of purpose, uniquely meant.

Embrace your calling, rise up, stand proud,

For in Christ, dear sister, you can stand out in the crowd.

Your journey is sacred, each moment a treasure,

With God as your anchor, your spirit will measure.

Colossians 3:2, set your sights on the skies,

For in the Father's embrace, true love never dies.

So take heart, dear woman, your destiny is near,

In the rhythm of your story, let hope steer.

With every heartbeat, let His truth shine bright,

You're destined to sparkle, a beacon of light.

Embrace your divine journey, let faith lead the way,

For in seeking His kingdom, you'll never stray.

With open hands and a heart that believes,

You'll discover hope and purpose in all He achieves.

Whispers from the Mountain

On the mountain high, where shadows softly fall,

Jesus speaks gently, a truth meant for all.

"Blessed are the meek," He calls with such grace,

"For they shall inherit this sacred place."

(Matthew 5:5)

"Come, weary souls, with burdens you bear,

My heart is a refuge; in Me, you'll find care."

The poor in spirit, He welcomes with love,

Their hope is renewed by the Father above.

(Matthew 5:3)

"Let your light shine brightly for all to see,

Reflecting My love, just as you're meant to be."

In every good deed, let kindness unfold,

A glimpse of My heart in the stories retold.

(Matthew 5:16)

He taught us to love, even those who oppose,

To turn the other cheek and let mercy flow.

"Forgive, and you'll find that forgiveness is key,

As I have forgiven, so must you be free."

(Matthew 6:14)

With wisdom so deep, He spoke of the heart,

"Where your treasure lies, there your soul will take part."

Seek first His Kingdom, and all will be yours,

His goodness and mercy will open new doors.

(Matthew 6:33)

"Do not be anxious; trust in My care,

Each day has enough; let Me lighten your wear."

He knows every need, each tear that we cry,

With love everlasting, He's always nearby.

(Matthew 6:34)

In the Beatitudes, we find our true call,

To live out His teachings, to love one and all.

Embrace the compassion that Jesus bestowed,

For in our surrender, His glory is shown.

(Matthew 5:7)

So, women of faith, rise up and take heart,

In the Sermon on the Mount, find your part.

With Jesus beside you, walk boldly each day,

In love and in grace, let His light be your way.

(Matthew 5:14)

Where Love Unbounds

In shadows deep where hearts reside,

A mother stood, her love the guide.

With every heartbeat, every breath,

She faced the cost, she met her death.

In a moment, fierce and true,

She gave her life, her dreams anew.

With courage strong, her spirit soared,

In love's embrace, her heart was poured.

As she whispered soft, "You are my light,"

She chose to battle the endless night.

In John 15:13, the truth unfolds,

"Greater love has no one than this," she holds.

Through trials vast and storms that roar,

She found her strength, she would not ignore.

In Romans 8:28, she stood secure,

For God works all things for good, that's pure.

Though loss may linger, sorrow may stay,

Her love will shine, it won't decay.

For every tear, in Psalm 30:5,

"Joy comes in the morning," she will thrive.

With each sacrifice, resilience grows,

A mother's love forever glows.

In 2 Corinthians 12:9, she finds her grace,

For His strength is made perfect in her embrace.

So rise, dear woman, with purpose bright,

Your journey, though hard, leads to the light.

Embrace your power, let love take flight,

For in sacrifice, you'll find your might.

As you walk forward, with faith as your guide,

Remember her love, let it be your pride.

In every heartbeat, let hope unfurl,

You are resilient, a daughter not of this world.

From Cocoon to Butterfly

In a small, quiet cocoon, a change begins,

Where dreams are wrapped tight and hope softly spins.

She waits in the stillness, dreaming of light,

Hoping for a future that feels just right.

Inside the cocoon, she's growing, unseen,

Transforming in ways she's never been.

Every struggle and shadow, every tear she's known,

Helps her prepare for the beauty that's shown.

From the tight cocoon, she'll break free with grace,

With bright, colorful wings and a smile on her face.

She'll spread out her wings, strong and bold,

Flying high and free, no longer controlled.

Her wings will shine in the sun's warm glow,

A beautiful sight for everyone to know.

She'll rise from the darkness, full of new light,

A butterfly soaring, truly a bold sight.

So as you come out from your own cocoon,

Embrace the new day and let your spirit bloom.

You'll fly like a butterfly, so bright and so true,

With confidence and beauty in everything you do.

Passport to Heaven

In the quiet of my heart, I found a sacred space,

A passport filled with promises, of love, and endless grace.

With every tear I've shed, each joy, each whispered prayer,

I've stamped my soul with courage, for I know He's always there.

The pages tell a story, of trials faced and won,

Of every step I've taken, guided by the Son.

Through storms that tried to break me, I held onto His hand,

My faith became my compass, as I walked through shifting sand.

In moments of confusion, when shadows loomed so near,

I opened up the Scriptures, and His voice became so clear.

"Fear not, for I am with you," echoed in my soul,

With every word a passport, leading me toward the goal.

The stamps of grace and mercy, each one a guiding light,

Reminding me of heaven, where darkness turns to bright.

No matter where I wander, no matter how far I roam,

This passport holds my purpose, for in Christ, I'm home.

So as I journey onward, through valleys and through peaks,

I carry this reminder, in my heart the truth speaks:

With faith as my foundation, and love that's ever true,

My passport leads to heaven, for His promise I pursue.

A Journey of Purpose

In the gentle glow of morning light,

She awakens with hope, her heart shining bright.

"For I know the plans I have for you," He proclaims,

Jeremiah 29:11, where love never wanes.

With every step she takes, she aims to embrace,

The calling on her life, filled with God's grace.

In Ephesians 2:10, her purpose is revealed,

A masterpiece in progress, His story unsealed.

With faith as her anchor, she walks on her way,

Guided by love, reflecting His sway.

"Seek first the Kingdom," Matthew 6:33 shows,
In all that she does, her true treasure grows.

For the joy of the Lord is her strength every day,
Nehemiah 8:10 brightens her way.
In trials and struggles, she knows she will stand,
With God by her side, she's safe in His hand.

As salt and as light, she shines ever bright,
Matthew 5:14, her purpose takes flight.
With compassion and grace, she reaches out wide,
Sharing His love, with the Spirit as guide.

She works with love, her heart open and free,
In every encounter, His love flows like the sea.
Colossians 3:23, in all that she does,
She serves the Lord, her passion, her cause.

With each act of kindness, she lifts up His name,
A reflection of Jesus, her heart set aflame.

"Let your light shine," so others may see,

The hope of the Gospel, alive in her plea.

So rise, faithful woman, live boldly inspired,

In the Kingdom of God, let your spirit be fired.

With purpose and passion, dance through each day,

In the arms of the Father, you'll find your way.

Becoming Love

In the stillness of her heart, she yearns to be,

The truest love, a reflection of Christ set free.

1 John 4:8 gently echoes within,

"For God is love," and thus her journey begins.

She strives to embody the love that He gave,

A selfless love, the kind that truly saves.

1 Corinthians 13:4-7 lights her way,

"Love is patient, love is kind," she chooses each day.

Not quick to anger, nor keeping a score,

Her heart expands beyond what it was before.

Romans 12:9 urges, "Let love be sincere,"

She sheds all pretenses, drawing her purpose near.

To love like Christ means embracing sacrifice,

Ephesians 5:2 calls her to walk in His light.

To live in love, as He laid down His life,

For her love to be pure, it must rise above strife.

She forgives those who've caused her pain, as He forgave her,

Colossians 3:13 reassures her spirit's stir.

Bearing with others, in peace and in grace,

She carries His love, transcending all race.

Her love becomes genuine when she lets herself fade,

Turning away from selfish desires and pride displayed.

Galatians 2:20 enlightens her soul,

"It is Christ who lives in me," making her whole.

Now she shines brighter, His love deep inside,

She loves the least, forgiving every stride.

In her heart, the Spirit guides her every move,

Revealing to the world what true love can prove.

And as she seeks to grow even more,

Her love deepens, its roots anchored in the Lord.

For in Christ, her love finds its rightful place,

A woman transformed by His mercy and grace.

50 Shades of Lipstick

In a world of vibrant colors, where dreams begin to bloom,

She opens up her treasure chest, dispelling any gloom.

A rainbow of emotions, in tubes both bold and bright,

Each shade tells a story, igniting day and night.

A sultry crimson whispers secrets of passion and fire,

While soft nude hues speak of comfort, sparking desire.

Corals dance like summer, with warmth that feels like sun,

And deep berry tones reflect the battles she has won.

With each application, she wears her heart on her sleeve,

A canvas of resilience, in shades that never deceive.

From playful pinks that giggle, to moody midnight blues,

Her lips become a palette, expressing all her views.

In matte or gloss, she embraces the stories that unfold,

Each layer a reminder of the fierce spirit she holds.

For every shade has meaning, a chapter of her life,

A testament of beauty, both in joy and strife.

Some days, she's vibrant, with a daring fuchsia smile,

Other times, she's subtle, opting for a more tender style.

In moments of reflection, she might reach for deep plum,

A reminder of the battles that brought her to this drum.

Fifty shades of lipstick, a journey through her soul,

A celebration of her power, a way to feel whole.

With every swipe, she finds strength, a voice that can't be missed,

For in each hue she chooses, she defines her own twist.

So here's to the lipstick, in shades both bold and shy,

To the stories it unlocks and the dreams that help her fly.

In every shade and shimmer, she embraces who she's meant,

With fifty shades of lipstick, her heart is truly bent.

From the Skyline

From the skyline, she gazes down below,

A world in motion, yet she feels so slow.

Life's rush beneath her, chaotic and fast,

But from the skyline, she finds peace at last.

The winds whisper stories through her hair,

Of trials faced, of burdens laid bare.

Yet in the height of her silent view,

She sees a horizon painted brand new.

Below, the noise of voices collide,

But up in the clouds, there's no need to hide.

From the skyline, her worries grow thin,

For here is where her healing begins.

She remembers the battles fought on the ground,

The scars she carries, though victory is found.

But from up high, they appear so small,

A distant echo of her courage's call.

The skyline offers a different sight,

A world so vast, drenched in morning light.

Her pain is still real, but her soul feels wide,

For in this space, she knows she'll survive.

She is more than the struggle, more than the fall,

From the skyline, she can see it all.

A life unfolding, shaped by grace,

As she rises above, to take her place.

From the skyline, her heart takes flight,

No longer bound by fear or fight.

She soars above, in faith so true,

Knowing her strength lies in the view.

And though the world may tremble below,

From the skyline, her spirit will grow.

A woman renewed, with wings outspread,

From the skyline, she moves ahead.

Kindness, Pass It On

In a world that often rushes, where hearts can feel cold,

A gentle smile can warm the soul, a story to be told.

With every act of kindness, a ripple starts to grow,

A seed of love planted deep, it's the light that we sow.

When life feels overwhelming, and shadows cloud the day,

A simple word of comfort can chase the dark away,

So let your heart be open, let compassion freely flow,

In the hands of one kind gesture, a brighter path can show.

Remember that each person carries burdens unseen,

A touch of grace can lighten the load, a bridge where hope has been.

When you lift another's spirit, you uplift your own too,

For kindness is a cycle, it circles back to you.

So take a moment, reach out, and let your heart respond,

In a world that needs connection, spread kindness—pass it on.

Together we can change the tides, make hearts feel like home,

In every act of kindness, no one has to be alone.

Brave Enough to Begin

She stood at the edge, bound by invisible chains,

In a world shaped by culture, tradition's reign.

They urged her to stay, to follow the line,

But deep in her heart, she sensed a sign.

For too long she'd adhered to the rules they laid,

Trapped by expectations that never seemed to fade.

Yet a fire within her started to ignite,

Whispering softly, "You were meant for more than this fight."

It wasn't in customs or traditions' hold,

Her hope, her purpose, they couldn't uphold.

In a realm of restrictions, she'd never discover

The freedom her spirit longed to uncover.

But with courage swelling, she took that leap,

Brave enough to abandon the life she'd keep.

Shattering the chains not just for her own,

But for countless others who felt all alone.

She walked toward freedom, toward the dawn,

With Jesus as her guide, she felt reborn.

In Him, she found the meaning she sought,

For it was in Christ her battles were fought.

Tradition grew quiet, culture lost its sway,

As she moved in freedom, day by day.

No longer shackled by the world's demands,

She entrusted her life into His loving hands.

And in that moment, she came to see,

Hope had never resided in what others decree.

It wasn't in the norms that held her down,

But in Jesus Christ, where her strength was found.

She was brave enough to start the fight,

Brave enough to step into the light.

And with each stride, she forged a path,

For others to find freedom, to feel the aftermath.

So to you, dear sister, who stands at the brink,

Know that freedom thrives in the heart that dares to think.

Be brave enough to take that first stride,

For in Christ alone, your purpose will abide.

Tethered for Life: I Think Not

In the depths of shadows, where whispers reside,

Life's burdens can feel like a heavy tide.

But, dear sister, listen to this truth,

You are not confined; you're filled with youth.

Each bruise tells a story, each scar a trace,

Not chains of despair, but marks that embrace.

You've weathered storms, fought battles with might,

With every tear shed, a lesson in sight.

Life may have tried to pull you down,

But the fire inside you continues to crown.

ECHOES OF RESILIENCE

Like a phoenix rising from ashes of strife,

You stand once more, stronger in life.

Tethered to hope, not sorrow or dread,

Each step you take, your purpose is spread.

You are a warrior, fierce and bright,

Claim your power, embrace your light.

So shake off the dust, stand tall and proud,

Let your heart sing, let your spirit shout loud.

For life may have bruised you, but it can't confine,

The strength in your soul, the will to climb.

You are not bound to a life filled with despair,

You're destined for greatness, beyond compare.

So rise, dear woman, let your spirit soar,

For you are a force; you are so much more.

In Overflow – A Forgotten Faucet

They left her there, abandoned and unseen,

Thinking her heart would run dry and lean.

Ignored and forgotten, like a shadowed dream,

Yet her spirit held fast, a quiet, fierce beam.

For love's gentle faucet, though left to flow free,

Overflowed with grace, a boundless decree.

With every whisper of the wind through the trees,

She felt the presence of love's gentle breeze.

Roots digging deeper, her faith took hold,

In the garden of grace, where her heart turned bold.

Each drop that cascaded told a story to share,

Of resilience and hope, of rising from despair.

Though the world may have deemed her empty and weak,

Her spirit sang songs of the joy she would seek.

The laughter of children danced in her mind,

A reminder that love is the light we can find.

Though abandoned by many, she'd never despair,

For in the quiet moments, she knew God was there.

Her heart was a vessel, a treasure untold,

Flowing with kindness, more precious than gold.

And those who had left, so quick to assume,

Would one day remember the light she'd consume.

As she moved forward, her purpose grew clear,

She'd shine for the lost, bringing hope and cheer.

In her overflow, she'd gather the broken,

With words of encouragement, love unspoken.

No longer tethered by the past that confined,

She danced through the shadows, a heart unaligned.

Her laughter a melody, her spirit a fire,

In the depths of her soul, she felt the desire.

To uplift the weary, the lonely, the lost,

To remind them of love, whatever the cost.

For her faucet was open, a divine intervention,

Filling the world with a heart's true intention.

So when you feel beaten, like hope's slipped away,

Remember the faucet that flows every day.

For even in darkness, love still can bloom,

And what once felt abandoned can fill every room.

Baggage Claim: Unchecked

She stood at life's terminal, weary and worn,

Carrying baggage from battles long fought.

Suitcases filled with regret and pain,

Each one heavier, soaked by the rain.

They told her, "Check it, leave it behind,"

But she clung tight, heart and mind.

Unwilling to let go of what once was,

Unsure if she could, or if she should, because—

Those bags became her identity,

Wounds that echoed her history.

The labels read "betrayed," "forgotten," "used,"

But beneath them all was a heart bruised.

Yet a whisper came, gentle and kind,

"Leave them here, they no longer define.

You're more than the weight you bear,

Let go, find freedom in My care."

But could she trust, could she believe,

That her past could fade and she could breathe?

With trembling hands, she took a stand,

Letting go wasn't easy, but it was planned.

At the claim, she left it all behind,

Every fear, every scar, each bind.

Unchecked, no longer hers to keep,

Freedom washed over, calm and deep.

Now she walks, her soul set free,

Lighter than ever, destined to be.

No baggage holds her captive still,

Her heart is whole, her spirit fulfilled.

For life's journey, she's learned this truth:

You can't move forward with burdens of youth.

To let them go is to truly live,

And in the end, it's grace we give.

Faithful Voices: A Tribute from the Throne Room

In the stillness of the morning, where hope starts to bloom,

Women gather in the throne room, their hearts dispelling gloom.

"Enter His gates with thanksgiving," as Psalm 100 states,

With every breath we take, we call upon His grace.

In this holy space, where praises fill the skies,

We lift our hands in worship, casting off our sighs.

"For I know the plans I have for you," the Lord does say,

Plans to prosper and not to harm, His promise lights our way.

Though trials may surround us, and storms may block our path,

We stand strong in His presence, embracing all His wrath.

"Be strong and courageous," He whispers soft and clear,

"For I am with you always, there's nothing left to fear."

As we bow before the throne, with burdens laid to rest,

We find our strength renewed, in His love, we are blessed.

"Cast all your cares on Him," for He cares for you so,

With every tear we shed, His grace begins to flow.

In the face of every battle, when doubt begins to creep,

We sing of His great faithfulness, our hearts, His promise keep.

"Do not fear, for I have redeemed you," Isaiah gently speaks,

"You are mine, I've called you by name," in His love, we find peace.

So let the waves come crashing, let the shadows try to stay,

We're warriors in His army, praising every day.

"For the joy of the Lord is our strength," Nehemiah reminds,

In the throne room of His presence, true hope we always find.

With every note of worship, we rise above the fray,

With hearts aligned in unity, we choose to praise today.

In the midst of every struggle, in the face of all despair,

We lift our voices higher, knowing He will always care.

So gather, dear women, in this throne room of grace,

With hearts set ablaze, let us seek His face.

For come what may, we'll praise Him loud and clear,

In the throne room of our Savior, there's nothing left to fear.

Personal Growth

THE JOURNEY TO YOUR TRUE SELF

Personal growth is the journey of becoming, a constant evolution where you shed old versions of yourself to step into who you're meant to be. It's a process filled with both painful lessons and beautiful revelations, an ongoing transformation shaped by every challenge, setback, and victory. For the women learning to embrace their flaws, strengths, and all the in-betweens—this is the unfolding of your true self.

Growth is a slow unfolding, a process of learning, healing, and discovering. In these poems, we explore the path of becoming—full of challenges and moments of clarity. As you read, embrace the beauty of change and the transformation that is always taking place within you.

In the Moment, Not for the Moment

I live each day as if it were my last,

Full of joy, no shadows cast.

Not for the fleeting spark of now,

But in this moment, where life allows.

No hours to waste, no time to claim,

I plunge into the depths, I never feign.

Once I struggled, but now I'm free,

To live simply, just to be.

My cup overflows, it does not cease,

With every step, I seek my peace.

The fear of death, I've let it go,

For in this life, I've found my flow.

With every breath, a gift, a grace,

Not a race to win, but a gentle pace.

I walk in calm, with no need to flee,

For in the present, I am truly me.

Blooming into Womanhood

In the quiet dawn of her early years,

A girl stands tall, confronting her fears.

With gentle petals, she begins to grow,

A world of dreams starts to flow.

Once a bud, timid and unsure,

Now she reaches for light, brave and pure.

Each struggle, a thorn; each tear, a dew,

Strength is rising, a spirit anew.

With every heartbeat, her story unfolds,

Of battles fought and courage bold.

She learns to dance in shadows and sun,

Finding her voice, ready to run.

Through fields of doubt, she walks with pride,

No longer hiding, she'll stand beside

The storms that life sends, she'll greet with grace,

For every ending leads to a new place.

With open hands, she shapes her fate,

Creating her world, refusing to wait.

In the tapestry woven of dreams yet untold,

She's the artist, the brave, the bold.

From girlhood whispers to womanhood's song,

She stands at the helm, where she belongs.

With passion ignited, she steps into the light,

Mastering womanhood, her future is bright.

So watch her rise, watch her bloom,

A flower unfolding, filling the room.

For she is the magic, the wild and the free,

Embracing her journey, her destiny.

Color me Purple

Color me purple, vibrant and bold,

A mix of heartache and hope to behold.

The blue of my struggles, the red of my fire,

Together they lift me, taking me higher.

In every hue, I discover my grace,

A royal shade that fills up my space.

Not too loud, nor timid and shy,

A color that helps my spirit to fly.

Paint me with courage, paint me with truth,

With wisdom that's grown from all of my youth.

In the glow of purple, I find my way,

Standing in strength, come what may.

Color me purple, rich and free,

The truest version of myself you'll see.

A soul that has found its rightful place,

In shades of purple, I rest in grace.

New Name – Same Heart

Once, a name defined me, a label on my skin,

Tied to who I used to be, where my journey had begun.

Through the echoes of my past, I wore my names like chains,

Each one a fleeting whisper of the losses and the gains.

I've changed my name more times than I can count,

Each new title like a cloak, a story to recount.

But beneath each layer woven, my essence still stays true,

A heart that beats for kindness, a spirit tried and blue.

In the mirror, I see the girl who faced the storms alone,

Each name a testament to battles I have known.

Yet as the world has shifted, like tides that ebb and flow,

I've held on to my anchor, the truth I've come to know.

For every new beginning, I've shed a piece of me,

But my heart remains untouched, a fierce tenacity.

I refuse to let them change me, to dim my inner spark,

For in the depths of who I am, lies beauty in the dark.

So here's to all the journeys, to the names I've left behind,

A tribute to the strength it takes to rise and to unwind.

With every name I carry, I celebrate my part,

For though they call me different, they can't change my heart.

Finding my Fire

In the heart of every woman, a spark lies awake,

A flame of resilience, ready to break.

Through trials and tempests, we rise and we fall,

Yet deep in our souls, we hear the call.

It begins as a flicker, a whisper, a light,

Guiding us gently through the long, dark night.

When doubt tries to smother, and fear takes its aim,

We breathe in our power, and we fan the flame.

Each challenge a lesson, each scar tells a tale,

Of strength in the struggle, of love that won't fail.

No storm can extinguish the fire that's ours,

We burn with the brilliance of countless stars.

With passion ignited, we stand firm and tall,

Embracing our journey, we answer the call.

For the fire within us is fierce and alive,

A beacon of hope, helping us thrive.

So gather your courage, let your heart be the guide,

Dance through the flames, let your spirit collide.

For we are the fire that cannot be tamed,

A force of pure magic, forever unclaimed.

With every step forward, we shine even brighter,

In the face of the shadows, we become our own lighter.

So let go of the doubt, rise up from the mire,

Embrace who you are, and find your own fire.

In the tapestry woven from struggles we bear,

We find strength in our stories, a truth we can share.

We're more than survivors; we're flames that inspire,

Together we stand, igniting the fire.

Head in Cages

In the corners of my mind, shadows twist and turn,

A maze of doubt and whispers, where the fires of hope burn.

I've walked through this prison, built by fear and blame,

Believing I was trapped, lost in a silent game.

Voices echoed loudly, telling me I'm small,

That my dreams were just fantasies, destined for a fall.

Each choice felt like shackles, each thought weighed me down,

In the cage of my own making, I wore a heavy crown.

But one day, a flicker, a spark deep inside,

A whisper of freedom, a chance to confide.

I looked through the bars, saw the world beyond,

Realized the cage was built by the thoughts I had donned.

With courage as my compass, I reached for the key,

Unlocking the chambers where I longed to be free.

Each breath a new beginning, each thought a fresh start,

I learned that my power was nestled in my heart.

The chains of perception began to break apart,

As I painted my journey, creating my art.

No longer confined, I emerged from the dark,

With my head held high, igniting my spark.

Now the world is wide open, the sky vast and clear,

No longer in cages, I've shed all my fear.

With each step I take, I choose to be bold,

For the freedom I've found is worth more than gold.

Layers Unfolded

Beneath the veil, she keeps herself concealed,

A woman of strength, though her heart is revealed.

Each layer tells a story, each fold bears a scar,

Beneath it all, she feels hidden so far.

Life's heavy burdens, like shadows, descend,

Yet her spirit stands tall, refusing to bend.

She sheds the weight, one tear at a time,

Unfolding her heart in a rhythm sublime.

The world may not grasp the depth of her soul,

But she walks with grace, still striving for whole.

For beneath the veil lies a truth yet untold,

A woman reborn as her layers unfold.

Each tear uncovers the strength she possesses,

A journey of self, in silence it blesses.

With every step, she discovers her grace,

Facing her fears, embracing the race.

The veil is lifted, her true self ignites,

A queen in her power, no longer in fright.

No longer hidden, no longer restrained,

She rises, unafraid, her worth now regained.

Beneath the veil, her beauty shines bright,

Her layers undone, she steps into the light.

What once was concealed, now boldly proclaimed,

She knows her worth, and walks unashamed.

Her Story, Her Strength

In a world where shadows whispered doubt,

She carried her story, refusing to pout.

Each chapter a struggle, each word a scar,

Yet deep in her heart, she knew just how far.

She walked through the fire, felt the burn on her skin,

But from every wound, she learned how to win.

With courage as armor, she faced every test,

Transforming her pain into purpose, her best.

Her story was woven with threads of the past,

Not a burden to bear, but a beacon steadfast.

She stood on the mountain of trials and tears,

And spoke with a voice that drowned out her fears.

"Here's my truth," she said, eyes shining bright,

"From darkness emerged an unyielding light.

What once felt like chains, now sets me apart,

Each piece of my journey is a map of the heart."

With every word spoken, she shattered the shame,

A tapestry stitched with both sorrow and flame.

She showed others pathways through valleys of dread,

That hope can arise where despair once had tread.

Her laughter was thunder, her spirit a breeze,

With grace, she transformed the hurt into ease.

Her story a lighthouse, guiding the lost,

Reminding them always of the beauty in cost.

For strength is not silent; it roars from within,

A chorus of voices, a melody's spin.

With her pen as a sword, she fought through the night,

Turning her struggles into stories of light.

So listen, dear sister, to the tale she unveils,

For within every struggle, her strength never fails.

Her story, her power, a gift to us all,

A reminder that rising is a choice, not a fall.

In the depths of her journey, she found her own grace,

And with every brave step, she embraced her own place.

Her story is strength; it sets hearts free,

A testament shining for you and for me.

Courageous Hearts

In a quiet corner where shadows used to play,

An abused little girl found a flicker, a way.

With chains of addiction looming near,

She envisioned a future where freedom was clear.

Through nights filled with sorrow, she whispered her plea,

"Lift me from darkness; help me to see."

In the depths of despair, she found her own light,

A spark of resilience igniting the night.

Courageous hearts beat louder than fear,

In the face of the storm, they refuse to disappear.

With each step she took on a path newly drawn,

She turned her pain into strength at dawn.

From the ashes of sorrow, she built a new dream,

An entrepreneur rising, her voice like a stream.

She traveled the world with a message so bright,

The gospel of hope, drawing souls to the light.

With every story shared, her heart would ignite,

A beacon of courage, shining so bright.

No longer a victim, she stood tall and proud,

Inspiring others, her voice like a crowd.

Her journey, a testament of love and grace,

A reminder that hope can be found in each place.

For the girl who was broken now holds the key,

Unlocking the hearts of those longing to be.

So let her be seen, let her story unfold,

For courageous hearts break the chains that once hold.

From darkness to light, she leads with her spark,

A guiding example, lighting up the dark.

With every new step, she dances through life,

Embracing the struggle, the joy, and the strife.

For the world needs her courage, her fire, her art,

A woman transformed with a courageous heart.

Coffee No Cure

She sat with her cup, steam rising slowly,

A morning ritual she had come to embrace.

The brew was bitter, as dark as her days,

But coffee, it seemed, couldn't clear the haze.

Her hands wrapped tightly around the mug,

Searching for warmth, a little love, a hug.

But no matter the flavor, whether strong or bold,

It couldn't chase away the nights so cold.

She thought a sip might ease the ache,

But the weight on her chest wouldn't break.

The caffeine buzz would soon wear off,

Leaving behind the worries she'd scoffed.

For life's deep wounds require more than a brew,

And no cup of coffee could pull her through.

Her heart longed for more than what beans could provide,

A reason, a purpose, a life to abide.

So she set down the cup, gazed at the sky,

Realizing coffee alone couldn't help her fly.

She needed hope, not just a drink,

A cure for the soul, a new way to think.

The remedy she sought wasn't in the cup,

But in rising again, learning to look up.

For within her heart, she held the key,

More than coffee—it was her destiny.

I Hold My Tongue

They called me crazy, whispered behind my back,

Doubt wrapped me in shadows, painted my world black.

I tried to speak, but no one would hear,

Their eyes full of judgment, their minds full of fear.

So I held my tongue, though my spirit burned bright,

Chose to live in silence, letting actions take flight.

In every step, I planted seeds of grace,

A quiet strength that no one could erase.

They saw madness, but I carried truth deep inside,

A storm that raged, yet I refused to hide.

Through the chaos, I stood tall, never lost sight,

Of the fire within me, still burning so bright.

No words could explain the battles I faced,

But I lived the proof, leaving no trace of disgrace.

Each move I made, each breath I took,

Was louder than any words I never spoke.

I walked through the storm, unseen but strong,

Living a testament where silence belonged.

Now they see me, not crazy or broken,

But the proof of the woman whose truth lived unspoken.

A Heart Forgiven – Peace Restored

I carried the weight, the guilt, and the pain,

A heart heavy with sorrow, caught in the rain.

I stumbled through darkness, lost in my thoughts,

Chained to the past, with no peace to be sought.

But in the stillness, a whisper came near,

A voice filled with mercy, gentle and clear.

"Let go of the burden, the wounds, the regret,

For a heart that's forgiven has no need to fret."

I fell to my knees, surrendered it all,

Each shattered piece, each rise and fall.

And as I let go, my spirit was renewed,

The chains fell away, and the light broke through.

A heart forgiven, the scars now erased,

Peace restored, in grace I embraced.

No longer held back by the shadows of yore,

I walk in the freedom of love evermore.

The storm has passed, the skies are now bright,

I breathe in the calm, with nothing in sight.

For a heart forgiven, by grace made anew,

Is a heart that finds peace, forever in view.

Daffodils So Bright

In the gentle embrace of spring's warm light,

Daffodils bloom, their petals so bright.

Golden trumpets, bold in their stance,

A symbol of womanhood, a vibrant dance.

With grace, they rise from the earth below,

Unfurling their beauty, letting their colors show.

Each flower tells a story, of strength and grace,

Resilient and hopeful, they find their place.

Like daffodils, women weather the storm,

Facing harsh winds, they embrace the warm.

With roots deep in courage, they stand tall and proud,

In the garden of life, they shine in the crowd.

Their laughter, like sunshine, spreads joy all around,

In every soft whisper, true love can be found.

With heads held high, they sway in the breeze,

Radiating warmth, putting hearts at ease.

Just as daffodils bring color to spring,

Women, too, are gifts that life's moments can bring.

They nurture the dreams that bloom in the night,

With kindness and passion, they set hearts alight.

So here's to the daffodils, resilient and bold,

In their essence, a woman's true spirit unfolds.

With each tender petal and every sweet sigh,

They teach us to flourish, to reach for the sky.

The Swingset of Womanhood

In the playground of life, where laughter plays,

The swingset of womanhood gently sways.

With every push, I rise to the sky,

Soaring high, embracing the reasons why.

I remember the first swing, the thrill of the ride,

Finding my balance, with courage as my guide.

The ups and the downs, the ebb and the flow,

Each moment a lesson, teaching me to grow.

With friends by my side, we'd take turns to fly,

Sharing secrets and dreams, letting worries pass by.

In the comfort of sisterhood, we'd laugh and we'd cry,

In the embrace of our stories, we learned to get by.

Yet, sometimes the swings would sway too fast,

With challenges rushing like shadows they cast.

When the world felt heavy, and doubts weighed me down,

I'd cling to the chains, refusing to drown.

For in each gentle swing, I found my voice,

A melody of strength, reminding me to rejoice.

I discovered my power in the rhythm and pace,

In the height of the swing, I found my place.

So I'll keep swinging, through storms and through sun,

Embracing the journey, knowing I've just begun.

In the swingset of womanhood, I'll always belong,

A dance of resilience, where my spirit is strong.

For with every heartbeat, I rise and I fall,

In the swingset of life, I can conquer it all.

So here's to the moments that make us who we are,

In the playground of womanhood, we'll always be a bright shining star.

Keyboard of My Heart

I sit here, fingers hovering above the keys,

The keyboard of my heart, where my thoughts are free.

Each note a feeling, each letter a word,

Telling stories no one's ever heard.

Some days, I type with joy and grace,

A melody of laughter, a peaceful place.

Other times, my fingers stumble and pause,

Caught in the tangles of life's sharp claws.

I've written love, I've written pain,

Lines of sunshine, verses of rain.

But no matter the rhythm, fast or slow,

It's my heart that leads, it's where I grow.

With each stroke, I find release,

In the noise of life, a quiet peace.

The world outside may rush and roar,

But here I find what I'm living for.

Every beat, every breath, a song unique,

The keyboard of my heart speaks what I seek.

No edits needed, no delete required,

Just raw truth, unmasked and inspired.

So I'll keep typing, through joy and strife,

Writing the story that is my life.

For in these keys, I've come to see,

The truest form of who I'm meant to be.

Days Gone By

I once looked back, wishing to remain,

Yearning for the comfort of the old refrain.

But the past had slipped, just out of reach,

While life pressed on, a lesson to teach.

Then I understood, in this moment right here,

Is where I truly exist, without fear.

The present is the key to unlock and see,

The person I'm destined to be.

No longer chasing what's left behind,

I've found my calm, I've cleared my mind.

Each moment is mine, I feel it expand,

And with it, I start to stand.

The future shines bright, here I reside,

Embracing the now, with arms open wide.

This is my time, my space to be,

For in the present, I am truly free.

A Woman in Red

In the midst of the crowd, she stands out bright,

A woman in red, glowing with light.

Her presence commands with a graceful air,

A symbol of strength in this vibrant affair.

With each step she takes, her intent is clear,

Unyielding and strong, she dispels all fear.

Her heart beats with courage, her eyes blaze with fire,

She knows who she is, and she's aiming higher.

Draped in her color, a mark of her might,

A champion for justice, she's ready to fight.

No hint of doubt can shake her resolve,

In the fabric of life, her spirit evolves.

With every word spoken, she sparks a new flame,

Leading with wisdom, she brightens the game.

A daughter of God, her mission in sight,

She carries her purpose, embracing the light.

Her confidence swells like the tide on the shore,

She knows her worth deeply, she's ready for more.

In a world that may try to dim her fierce glow,

She shines with the truth that she's destined to show.

For the woman in red is a sight to behold,

A tale of hope, of passion, of bold.

She walks with conviction, unshaken, unbent,

A beacon of promise, a life well-spent.

So here's to the woman who walks in her power,

Draped in red beauty, like a blooming flower.

With a heart full of purpose, she soars through the skies,

In her journey of faith, watch her rise and surprise.

Love's True Power: Still I Choose

He tried to break me, piece by piece,

With words like chains, a heavy leash.

His hands, they scarred, his lies like fire,

But deep within, rose something higher.

Each tear I shed, each silent cry,

Felt like my soul was set to die.

But in that pain, I found a flame,

A spark of strength that bore no shame.

His hate was loud, his rage so clear,

Yet something sacred drew me near.

It wasn't fear, nor bitter fight—

It was the dawn of my inner light.

For every strike that sought to kill,

A love within grew stronger still.

The more he tore, the more I found

A grace in me that stood its ground.

He sought to strip away my soul,

But in those shards, I became whole.

What he destroyed, I used to build—

A heart with love, not hate, fulfilled.

I found my purpose through the pain,

To break the cycle, break the chain.

To lift with love, where hate had been,

And show the world where hope begins.

I'll live my truth, I'll walk with grace,

And leave behind the dark embrace.

For love, not hate, shall be my sword,

It's in my spirit, and in the Lord.

What tried to crush me made me free,

Revealed the strength inside of me.

Now I stand tall, with heart so pure,

I live in love—my soul is sure.

I Toyed with You

In shadows deep, where secrets lie,

I danced with whispers, letting them fly.

A tempting call, so sweet, so sly,

I toyed with you, not asking why.

You wrapped around me, soft as a sigh,

With every promise, you made me high.

In your embrace, I thought I'd thrive,

But beneath your charm, you aimed to contrive.

Each fleeting thrill, a moment's delight,

Yet darkness crept in, veiling the light.

I played with fire, thought I could win,

But the flames consumed me, deviling sin.

You painted my world in colors so bold,

But left me with ashes, my spirit sold.

Each laugh turned to tears, each joy to despair,

In the game of your making, I was unaware.

Yet in the wreckage, a spark remained,

A flicker of hope through all that I'd gained.

For with every toy, there lies a choice,

And from the ashes, I reclaim my voice.

No longer a pawn in your wicked game,

I rise from the ruins, unashamed of my name.

For though I once toyed, now I stand true,

In the light of redemption, I break free from you.

With lessons learned, I'll forge my own way,

No more a puppet to lead me astray.

Deviling sin, I've closed the door,

In the arms of forgiveness, I'm lost nevermore.

I Made My Bed, Now What?

I made my bed, soft sheets pulled tight,

In the quiet of dawn, as night fades from sight.

The world claims this act is the key to success,

But all I see now is a tangled mess.

Laundry awaits, a mountain of clothes,

Dishes in the sink, where the water still flows.

I scrubbed and I cleaned, yet chaos remains,

Why did no one warn me success comes with strains?

Each wrinkle I smooth feels like a race,

But the clutter around me steals my heart's grace.

They said, "Make your bed, and the rest will align,"

Yet here I am wondering, "Where's the finish line?"

My heart bears the weight of expectations unspoken,

While the dreams that I cherish feel shattered and broken.

The list of to-dos stretches endlessly wide,

And I'm left here pondering, "Where do I hide?"

Am I a success when the chaos won't cease?

Is the clutter I battle robbing me of peace?

With each passing moment, I question my worth,

In a world full of noise, I long to give birth—

To the dreams I once held, the passions I crave,

But it's hard to find strength when I'm caught in the wave.

Yet as I look closer, I start to unsee,

That this mess is my journey, my growth, and my plea.

For success isn't measured by beds neatly made,

But by love that I offer, by joy I've displayed.

Though dishes may pile, and the laundry's not done,

I'm weaving a life where my heart's work has spun.

I rise from the chaos, embracing the fray,

In the mess and the madness, I'll find my own way.

For each challenge I face is a step toward the light,

And in the heart of my home, I'll continue to fight.

So, what comes next, you might ask with a sigh,

It's the strength of the weary, the heart that won't die.

I'll find joy in the journey, in all that I do,

For I made my bed, and I'll rise anew.

Deal with the Devil: Canceled

In shadows she lingered, a deal in her hand,

A glimmer of promise, a life well planned.

She traded her soul for a taste of the sweet,

Believing the devil could make her complete.

He whispered of fortune, of power and pride,

With each passing moment, she felt him beside.

But as days turned to nights, the price became clear,

The devil was cunning, feeding on fear.

With chains that were hidden, he tightened his hold,

What seemed like a dream now felt dark and cold.

Her heart ached with longing, her spirit felt weak,

For the devil, it seemed, had more than she'd seek.

She stood on the edge, a vast drop ahead,

With a heart full of hope, she refused to be led.

In the depths of despair, a spark flickered bright,

She knew at that moment she had to fight.

"Enough is enough," she declared with resolve,

No longer a pawn, she was ready to evolve.

With courage, she severed the ties that had bound,

No longer a victim, her freedom was found.

"I cancel this deal," she boldly proclaimed,

No more would she live in a life filled with shame.

The darkness receded, the light filled her soul,

As she stepped into grace, becoming made whole.

She sought out her Savior, the One who redeems,

In the arms of the Father, she found all her dreams.

An unbreakable covenant, forever she'd stand,

With love that was pure, guided by His hand.

No longer tethered to shadows or lies,

She embraced her true worth, and her spirit would rise.

In the freedom she found, she became all she'd lost,

For the path to true joy is worth any cost.

Now she walks with the light, leaving darkness behind,

Her heart filled with love, her spirit aligned.

A deal with the devil? She turned it away,

For the grace of her Savior shines brighter each day.

A Common Current

In a sea of voices and noise, we navigate,

Chasing dreams, reaching for fleeting joys.

We wish, we wonder, we hope—but remain unsure,

Lost in confusion, seeking what is pure.

A common current flows through us all,

A thread of truth that answers the call.

Yet we drift, distracted, swaying side to side,

Overshadowed by doubts we strive to hide.

But at the center, there's a place of peace,

Where clarity reigns, and truth finds release.

We tap into the current, deep and wide,

A wisdom we've always held, but kept inside.

No need to waste years chasing after the breeze,

When wisdom awaits, just look within with ease.

It's found in the stillness, the quiet, the calm,

A current of knowing, a soothing balm.

Stop wandering aimlessly, chasing shadows in vain,

Centralize your heart, step out of the rain.

The common current flows steady and sure,

A path to the peace that will always endure.

No more confusion, no more delay,

Just knowing, just being, day after day.

The answers were there, not far, but near,

In the common current, so bright and clear.

So ground yourself in what you already know,

Let the truth of the current guide you home.

No more guessing, no more despair,

Just a life lived fully, intentional and aware.

In the Know

We see the world, its symbols so clear—

A swoosh, a bite, we know who's near.

Man-made logos, bold and bright,

Instantly recognized in the blink of light.

But beyond the brands, the fame, the show,

Is there a symbol we truly know?

Unspoken, unseen by earthly design,

Yet it stands eternal, forever divine.

The symbol of Jesus, the cross, His grace,

A mark of love no time can erase.

Unseen by many, yet felt by all,

A symbol that lifts when we start to fall.

To wear His love, to carry His name,

Is to walk in power, unbound by fame.

Not for profit, not for gain,

But to reflect a love that heals all pain.

In a world full of idols, fleeting and fast,

There's one symbol of love that will always last.

Not printed, not sold, not in flashing lights,

But etched in hearts, where love ignites.

To be His symbol, to stand and show,

That love is real, and mercy flows.

We don't need billboards, don't need gold,

Just hearts that live the truth we hold.

In the stillness, in the quiet, it's there—

A symbol of love, of peace, of prayer.

It's unspoken, yet echoes loud and clear,

A mark of hope that casts out fear.

So let us be His living sign,

Reflecting love in all that shines.

For His symbol of grace will never fade,

It's eternal, pure, and perfectly made.

No brand, no logo, no worldly glow,

Can match the love we come to know.

Unspoken, yet present, with power untold,

The symbol of Jesus—our hearts to hold.

Afterword

As you reach the end of this collection, I hope you've found echoes of your own journey within these pages—moments of resilience, hope, and personal growth that resonate with the heart of who you are. Life is filled with ups and downs, but it's in those very moments of uncertainty and struggle that we learn the most about ourselves. These poems were written for the woman who has questioned her worth, who has faced the unknown with trembling hands, and who continues to rise each day with a quiet strength she may not always recognize.

You are not alone in your search for identity and purpose. Through every challenge and triumph, you are constantly evolving into a truer version of yourself. I hope this collection has served as a reminder that no matter where you are in your journey, there is always light ahead. Keep embracing your growth, nurturing your hope, and honoring the resilience within you.

Thank you for allowing these words to accompany you on this part of your path. May they continue to inspire and support you in the days to come.

With love and gratitude,
Rebekah Hope

About the author

Rebekah Hope is a Certified Life Coach dedicated to empowering women in their twenties to discover and live out their true purpose. Her journey has been marked by profound challenges—after being exiled from her Amish family at the age of 17, Rebekah became a two-time suicide survivor and managed to escape a three-year marriage characterized by domestic violence. These life experiences have shaped her into the coach she is today, passionate about guiding others toward hope, healing, and a purposeful life.

In 2019, Rebekah published her autobiography, *Beyond the Brokenness*, a book that has reached readers in over 10 countries, including India, Asia, and Germany. Through her writing, public speaking at suicide prevention events, and unwavering support for victims of domestic violence and mental illness, Rebekah has made it her mission to share the message that there is always hope, no matter how dark life may seem.

As the founder of the Divine Hope Community, Rebekah works with women who feel lost or stuck, helping them reconnect with their purpose and value. She believes that every woman has a unique voice and a divine purpose, and her goal is to provide the tools, resources, and community support needed to help them step into a transformed way of living.

If you or someone you know is struggling with mental health challenges or is trapped in a domestic abuse situation, Rebekah invites you to join her free Facebook community or reach out to her personally. She is committed to helping others find hope and build a life that reflects their true potential.

Rebekah's Motto: *"Do what you can, with what you have, from where you are, because there is HOPE FOR ALL!"*

More Info: https://linktr.ee/rebekahhope

Contact Rebekah: https://calendly.com/rebekah-divinehope

www.ingramcontent.com/pod-product-compliance
Lightning Source LLC
LaVergne TN
LVHW010952240225
804297LV00004B/5